Herbal Kombucha

Super Easy and Delicious Kombucha Recipes to Boost Your Immune System

Kevin Curt

© **Copyright 2020 - All rights reserved.**

The content contained within this book may not be reproduced, duplicated or transmitted without direct written permission from the author or the publisher.

Under no circumstances will any blame or legal responsibility be held against the publisher, or author, for any damages, reparation, or monetary loss due to the information contained within this book, either directly or indirectly.

Legal Notice:

This book is copyright protected. It is only for personal use. You cannot amend, distribute, sell, use, quote or paraphrase any part, or the content within this book, without the consent of the author or publisher.

Disclaimer Notice:

Please note the information contained within this document is for educational and entertainment purposes only. All effort has been executed to present accurate, up to date, reliable, complete information. No warranties of any kind are declared or implied. Readers acknowledge that the author is not engaged in the rendering of legal, financial, medical or professional advice. The content within this book has been derived from various sources. Please consult a licensed professional before attempting any techniques outlined in this book.

By reading this document, the reader agrees that under no circumstances is the author responsible for any losses, direct or indirect, that are incurred as a result of the use of the information contained within this document, including, but not limited to, errors, omissions, or inaccuracies.

Table of contents

INTRODUCTION 1

How Is Kombucha Made? 2

Fermentation Process 3

CHAPTER 1: WHY HERBAL KOMBUCHA? 4

CHAPTER 2: HERBAL KOMBUCHA HEALTH BENEFITS .. 5

Gut Health 6

Detoxifies the Body 7

Anti-Aging Benefits 8

Improved Immunity 9

Elevates Mood 10

Energizing Properties 11

CHAPTER 3: CHOOSING HERBS FOR YOUR HERBAL KOMBUCHA 12

Herbs High in Essential Oils 13

Artificial Flavors 14

Dried Herbs 15
    How to Dry Fresh Herbs 16

Your Kombucha Culture 17

General Rules 17

CHAPTER 4: HOW TO MAKE HERBAL KOMBUCHA 18

Things You Need to Get Started 19

Before You Start 19
    No Mold 20
    Stay Away from Plastic and Metal Containers 20
    Focus on the Temperature 20
    Keep Everything Clean 20

Kombucha Processes 21

Step One: Making the SCOBY 22
    Brewer's Notes 23

Step Two: First Fermentation 25
    Brewer's Notes 26

Third Step: Second Fermentation Process 27
    Brewer's Notes 28

Kombucha Making FAQ 29

CHAPTER 5: SUPER EASY AND DELICIOUS HERBAL KOMBUCHA RECIPES 30

Herbal Blends for Health 30
    Dandelion, Nettle, Yarrow, Raspberry Leaves, and Elderflower 31
    Ginger Root and Asian Pear 33
    Green Tea, Rosehip Peels, and Nettle Leaves 35
    Yarrow, Lycopod, Dandelion, and Nettle 37
    Cinnamon, Rosehip, and Elderberry 39
    Woodruff, Yarrow, Dandelion, Nettle Leaves, and Chickweed 41

Strawberry Leaves, Blackberry Leaves, Raspberry Leaves, and Black Currant Leaves 43

Fruit-Infused Herbal Drinks 45
   Basil and Strawberry Kombucha 46
   Ginger and Blueberry Kombucha 48
   Mint and Peach Kombucha..50
   Kombucha Lemonade..52
   Rosemary and Citrus Kombucha 54
   Spiced Pear 56

Kombucha Smoothies..58
   Honey and Ginger Smoothie...59
   Go for Green Smoothie 61
   Berry, Banana, Jasmine, and Lavender Smoothie 63
   Ginger, Thyme, and Blueberry Smoothie 65
   Apple and Dandelion Smoothie 67

Leftover SCOBY Recipes...69
   Cookie Dough 69
   Probiotic Energy Balls..71
   Garlic Dressing 73
   SCOBY Popsicles 74

Herbal Kombucha Cocktails 76
   Vodka Kombucha Zinger...76
   Moscow Mule 77
   Cranberry Mule 78

CONCLUSION...80

Introduction

Way back when, the drink kombucha was only found in cafes for hipsters and the health-conscious. Times have since then changed and now kombucha is a regular feature on most, if not all restaurant menus and have found a place on the shelves of supermarkets.

Kombucha has a unique taste and depending on what has been added to it to alter the taste, it can sometimes be described as a cider-tasting drink.

Kombucha dates back 2200 years ago to when the Chinese consumed it for its various health benefits which include both energizing and detoxifying properties. When trade routes began to emerge, kombucha traveled to Russia and then other European countries.

When WWII broke out, it found a place in Germany and in the 1950s it became a frequented drink for both North Africans and the French. By the 60s scientists from Switzerland claimed that the drink held remarkable health benefits and was beneficial for the gut.

How Is Kombucha Made?

Kombucha is traditionally made from a black or green tea base. A fermented white sugar is added which has been cultured using a tea fungus called a SCOBY (Symbiotic Culture of acetic acid Bacteria and Yeast).

Tastes may vary from a tangy taste in the early stages of fermentation to a vinegary taste in the later stages of fermentation.

The process of fermentation is pivotal, as SCOBY alters the polyphenols (compounds found in vegetables, fruits, and tea) into other organic compounds. This ups the acidity and stops microorganisms from growing. During the fermentation process, the drink can form a mushroom-like covering over the surface, thus kombucha is also known as "mushroom tea". SCOBY can be used to go on and ferment new batches of kombucha too.

It is this newly formed organic compound that is said to promote health and wellness above and beyond those that are already present in black and green tea.

Fermentation Process

When kombucha is fermented, it automatically extends its shelf life. Similar to other more commonly found fermented products like wine, beer, yogurt, and cheese.

The alcohol content in wine and beer occurs and increases during the fermentation process. Kombucha on the other hand only contains 0.5% alcohol. Countries such as New Zealand and Australia class drinks below this average as non-alcoholic. There are options however that hold a higher alcohol percentage and you will have to be over the age of 21 in order to purchase them.

Kombucha is not the answer to all your medical problems but does have many benefits that can support your overall health and wellness, thanks to the fermentation process.

Some may find that drinking kombucha is an acquired taste because of its tartness, so the best way forward is to sample a few and find the ones you enjoy drinking to include in your everyday life.

Chapter 1: Why Herbal Kombucha?

Foods that have gone through some form of a fermentation process and that gain probiotic properties through this process come with a range of health benefits which include improving digestion and gut health. They also lend themselves to creating and balancing your gut microbiome that positively impacts many other areas of your health.

Kombucha may potentially lessen the inflammation within the gut and release antioxidants. Anybody looking to improve their health should also note that drinking kombucha does not replace eating a healthy and varied diet either.

Kombucha is also rich in vitamin B, may lend itself to weight-loss, and can improve inflammation.

Other reasons why you should consider adding it to your diet are because it:

Supports those who may be vitamin-deficient.

Ups your memory.

Helps maintain and strengthen your hair, nails, and skin.

Guards against developing chronic illness.

Chapter 2: Herbal Kombucha Health Benefits

There are so many listed benefits of drinking kombucha, here we take a look at some of the main areas of your health that it can support and benefit.

Gut Health

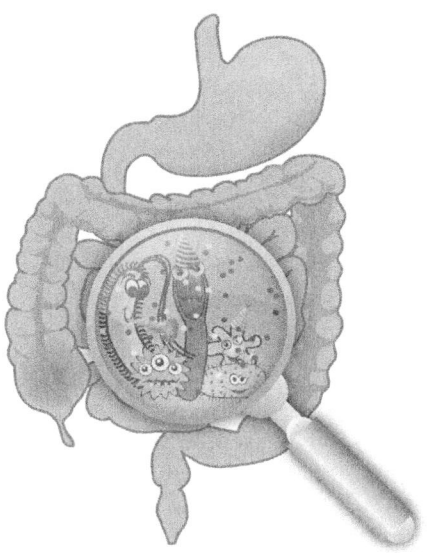

As kombucha undergoes a fermentation process it means that it is rich in probiotics. This bacteria is alike to the good bacteria found within your gut. Consuming a diet that is high in probiotics does improve your overall gut health. (Leonard as cited by Medical News Today, 2019)

Probiotics are also known to help treat irritable bowel syndrome and more commonly, diarrhea.

More research is being done to determine the impact kombucha has on the gut but the link between immunity and gut health is improved through the intake of probiotics is known and supported. Therefore drinking kombucha is ideal in helping you to balance your gut and improve your immune system.

Detoxifies the Body

Kombucha is rich in antioxidants, particles which fight free-radicals (molecules that can harm your cells). Scientists are quick to suggest that it is better to get your antioxidants in through the foods you consume that from supplements.

A green tea-based kombucha shows significant effects on the liver which can help lower levels of toxicity with the liver. It is also known to decrease this level by more than 70%. (Leech as cited by Healthline, 2018) Human trials have not begun specifically related to this area of research but are shown to be a field of promise.

Green tea is known to contain rich antioxidant properties and bioactive compounds such as polyphenols. Apart from its powerful antioxidant properties, research has indicated that green tea may help you burn more calories, lower cholesterol, and control your blood sugar levels (Efficacy of a Green Tea Extract Rich in Catechin Polyphenols and Caffeine in Increasing 24-h Energy Expenditure and Fat Oxidation in Humans as cited by National Library of Medicine, 1999).

Anti-Aging Benefits

When we age our skin cells begin to break down, leaving you prone to developing wrinkles, loose skin, and sagging. Kombucha holds powerful antioxidants in particular EGCGs that are 20 times more powerful than attacking and fighting off free radicals than vitamin C. EGCGs have a high moisture retention rate that stops your skin from aging and the formation of wrinkles.

Improved Immunity

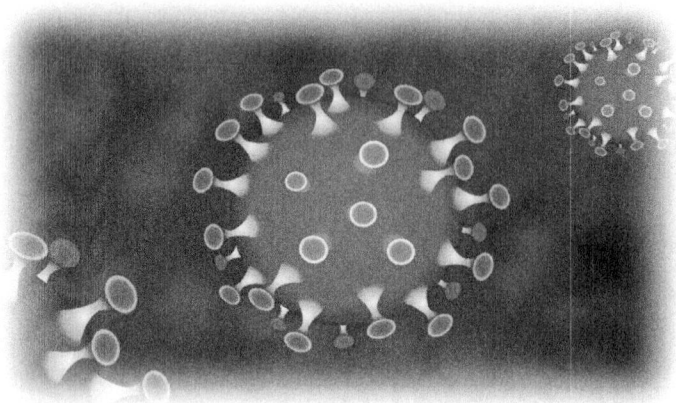

Another substance that is produced during the fermentation process of making kombucha is acetic acid. Vinegar is just as rich in this acid as vinegar is. Acetic acid is known to kill many harmful microorganisms which can hamper your health.

Kombucha fights off candida yeasts and infection-causing bacteria. The antimicrobial effect stops these bacteria from growing and spreading throughout the body and also prevents this before the body has a chance to absorb the bad bacteria.

Kombucha is also said to be high in vitamin C and DSL both of which guard against inflammatory disease, cell damage, and tumors.

Elevates Mood

Drinking kombucha may help elevate your mood. This is because there is a known link between probiotics in the gut and its influence over depression. Depression and inflammation are notoriously linked to one another and therefore the anti-inflammatory properties of kombucha may help ease some of the symptoms of depression.

Vitamins B1, B6, and B12 are all found in kombucha and can help increase levels of concentration, kick depression, and stabilize moods. Vitamin C is also found in kombucha and is known to prevent the release of the cortisol (stress hormone) from flooding the body.

Scientists have determined that there is strong evidence to suggest that probiotics can help stave off depression. (Milev and Wallace as cited by NCBI, 2017).

Energizing Properties

In addition to the traces of caffeine found in kombucha, it can contain high amounts of iron and vitamin B. Iron fuels the hemoglobin within our bloodstreams which increases the flow of oxygen through our bodies.

Some brew kombucha solely for its energizing properties and hence you may find more energy-enhancing kombucha drinks at the supermarket than other varieties targeting other benefits.

Athletes are also beginning to talk about the benefits of drinking kombucha not just for its energy-boosting ingredients but also because it plays an important role in recovery after strenuous exercise. Soviet Union athletes were said to drink one quart per day to stop the aches and pains associated with the lactic acid buildup in the muscles.

Chapter 3: Choosing Herbs for Your Herbal Kombucha

Brewing your own kombucha that is made using herbal or fruit teas is easier than many would come to believe.

Many people choose to make kombucha using herbal tea to avoid the caffeine content or to reap the many medical benefits that herbs carry.

Many may choose to use herbs to alter the flavor and aroma of their kombucha too and it offers an exciting twist when making your kombucha, as it leaves you room to experiment.

There are so many varieties of herbal teas available that you may become confused as to which are the correct ones to buy to brew your kombucha.

If you follow the below-mentioned tips of what to consider when brewing herbal kombucha you will be well on your way to creating a tasty and healthy batch of kombucha.

Herbs High in Essential Oils

Essential oils with a strong aroma can hamper the growth of your kombucha. Stay away from herbs such as peppermint, orange peel, caraway, mint, lemon peel, aniseed, and ginger.

Mint is often hard to avoid in most herbal mixes but if you do want to add a very small pinch of it should not harm your SCOBY or fermentation process. As a guide, if you buy mixtures of herbs or herbal tea, mint should appear as the fourth or fifth ingredient in the list for it to be ok to use.

Artificial Flavors

Often large manufacturers tend to add artificial aromas to their herbal teas and are often then sold with very whimsical names like "Christmas Tot" or "Tropical Heat". There are a large number of people who believe they are drinking herbal tea for their health but completely unaware that they are drinking herbal teas made with interchangeable and inferior herbs, and flavored with artificial aromas. Therefore one would question if they are actually as good as they say they are when supporting your health.

When brewing kombucha, the likelihood of it being a success will also rely on you using organic, wholesome ingredients. SCOBY is just as sensitive toward those herbal teas flavored with artificial substances, and you may notice that it does not ferment or grow as it should within the recommended time frame.

Always read the label when purchasing herbal teas to make sure that what they say is in the box is the true ingredient and not mixed with any other inferior ingredients and flavorings. If you come across ingredients that read "flavor" but do not contain the word "natural" then you know that what you have in your hand is not the real deal.

Dried Herbs

If you made your own herbal mixture or if you bought a store-bought mixture, ensure that your herbs are thoroughly dry before using them. Fresh ingredients do contain microspores which can alter the fermentation process and may even contaminate your SCOBY.

How to Dry Fresh Herbs

Air drying is the most effective method when it comes to drying herbs. This is ideal for herbs which do not contain high moisture content such as thyme, rosemary, dill, bay leaves, marjoram, and oregano.

To ensure that the herbs retain their flavor you need to allow them to dry naturally or if you do have one, use a food dehydrator. Alternatively, you can set your oven on low heat and dry the herbs in this manner.

If you are looking to preserve herbs with a higher moisture content such as tarragon, basil, mint or chives you may consider using a food dehydrator too.

Follow these instructions to help further dry your herbs and flowers:

Air Drying

Collect your herbs and flowers and tie the end with an elastic band or string. If the bundle is kept small they will dry faster.

Place the herbs, stem side up, in a brown paper bag. Then tie up the end of the bag. Use a toothpick to create a few small holes to serve as ventilation.

Handle the bags by their stems in a warm, ventilated room.

Your herbs will have to be stored in an airtight container within a week.

Oven Drying

Place your herbs and flowers onto a piece of baking parchment and onto a baking tray.

Set them in your oven to bake at 180°F for two to four hours. If the leaves appear crumbly then they are ready to be removed and stored in an airtight container for future use.

Remember that oven drying is known to remove a bit more of the flavor and aroma from herbs, you may be tempted to use a bit more when making your herbal kombucha tea.

Your Kombucha Culture

If you are trying the recipe out for the first time, pay careful attention to your culture. You may notice that the fungus has stopped growing. To be on the safe side, always make a second batch of SCOBY using plain black tea as a reserve. If the SCOBY stops growing in the herbal tea, you can transfer it to the black tea mixture. You may choose to mix the two teas, with a combination of either 25% to 50% green or black tea, as these teas are ideal for the tea fungus to grow.

General Rules

The amount of herbal tea or loose herbs, and flowers should be double that of regular tea, for example, 0.5 ounces per 34 fl. ounces.

Always make your kombucha with fresh, filtered water.

Chapter 4: How to Make Herbal Kombucha

No more having to buy store-bought kombucha. Now you invest in your health and make it yourself in the comfort of your own home. The first few times you make kombucha may prove tricky but once you know what to look out for you will become a top brewer.

Things You Need to Get Started

Below is a list of items that you may consider to help you get started.

- **Starter kit:** These can be purchased online and often come with an already made pack of SCOBY.
- **Black tea:** Black tea forms the base of your kombucha.
- **Starter tea:** You may consider purchasing a store-bought starter tea or use your home-brewed kombucha to start your various batches.
- **Flip-top fermentation bottles:** These bottles can seal tightly and are created to keep the carbonation in.
- **Ceramic container or jars:** Make sure you have one that can hold over one gallon. Or two glass jars that hold half a gallon each.
- **Cheesecloth:** This allows your kombucha mix to breathe while undergoing the fermentation. It also keeps bugs and dust away.
- **Elastic bands:** This is to seal your jars.

Before You Start

Before you begin you may want to consider the following to ensure that you make an unforgettable kombucha the first time around.

No Mold

If you at any time noticed that mold is beginning to form on your SCBOY or possibly in the tea then get rid of your batch immediately. You can tell if it is mold by its color, either green, black or white.

Stay Away from Plastic and Metal Containers

Both metal and plastic can cause an unwanted reaction when it comes to your SCOBY and the storing of your kombucha. The metal reacts badly to kombucha and may ruin you SCOBY. Plastic may accommodate harmful bacteria, something you do not want when making your beloved health drink.

Focus on the Temperature

The fermentation process can be sped up by warmer climates and will slow down when the temperature dips.

Keep Everything Clean

To keep away the bad bacteria it is important to keep everything clean, including your work station. Bad bacteria can make you fall ill and leave you feeling terrible.

Kombucha Processes

Here is a short overview of the various steps and periods when it comes to making Kombucha.

- SCOBY takes between one and four weeks to make the "mother" batch.
- The first fermentation process will take between six and ten days to make the kombucha.
- The second fermentation process will take three to ten days and this allows the kombucha to become carbonated.

Step One: Making the SCOBY

Ingredients:

- Elastic bands
- Cheesecloth
- Ceramic jug that can hold one gallon or two glass jars made to hold half a gallon each
- 7 cups water
- 4 bags black tea, or 1 tbsp loose leaf black tea
- ½ cup white sugar
- 1 cup unflavored, unpasteurized, store-bought kombucha.

Directions:

1. In a large saucepan over high heat bring the water to a boil. Once boiled remove from the heat and stir in the sugar until it has dissolved.
2. Add the tea and allow it to steep. Steep the tea until the water has cooled down to room temperature.
3. Transfer the tea into the ceramic jug or two jars. Then pour the store-bought kombucha over the top of the tea evenly. Include all the small pieces that may be lodged at the bottom of the store-bought kombucha

too. These are important to add to the jars if there are any.

4. Cover the mouth of the jug or jars with a few tightly woven layers of cheesecloth, secure with the elastic bands.
5. Place the jars in a dark area which is room temperature. Store this for one to four weeks until you notice a ¼ inch SCOBY has formed on top of the tea.
6. Keep the SCOBY in the original tea until you are ready to brew your first batch of kombucha. When you use SCOBY, be sure to toss the starter tea used to make it and do not use it during your first round of fermentation.

Brewer's Notes

Here are a few things to keep in mind when you are making your SCOBY.

- If you divide this recipe between two half a gallon jars you can make two SCOBYs. You can make more but be sure to follow the proportions and listed ingredients as mentioned, no adding extra sugar or water for example.
- If you have enough SCOBY and enjoy making fresh batches when brewing kombucha, why not consider making gummy candies?

- When buying any tea for your kombucha make sure it is not decaffeinated. The SCOBY does not grow as rapidly as it should when made using decaf tea.
- Whatever you do, do not tamper with the bottle while it is resting. Do not shake it or stir it, leave it be and it will naturally do what it is meant to do.
- When making SCOBY, first start by using black tea as the SCOBY tends to grow less when made with green and fruit teas.
- Do not substitute the sugar for honey or include honey during this process. Honey contains bacteria called botulism which can be dangerous. You are welcome to add honey in the second fermentation process when enough good bacteria are present to fight off the bad bacteria.

Step Two: First Fermentation

Now that you have made the SCOBY you can make your kombucha.

Ingredients:

- Elastic bands, Cheesecloth
- Ceramic jug that can hold one gallon or two glass jars made to hold half a gallon each
- 1 SCOBY or more depending on how many jars you are using
- 14 cups water
- 1.5 to 1.8 oz. dried herbs, or 8 bags green or black tea, or 2 tbsp loose leaf tea
- 1 cup white sugar
- 2 cups unflavored, store-bought kombucha

Directions:

1. In a large saucepan over high heat bring the water to a boil. Once boiled remove from the heat and stir in the sugar until it has dissolved.
2. Add the dried herbs or tea and allow it to steep. Steep the herbs or tea until the water has cooled down until room temperature.
3. Wash your hands then remove your SCOBY from the jar and transfer it onto a clean plate. Throw the old tea mixture away.

4. Pour the new tea mixture (strain if using loose leaf tea or herbs) into the jar(s) followed by the store-bought kombucha.
5. Transfer the SCOBY to the fresh jar(s).
6. Cover the mouth of the jar(s) with a few layers of cheesecloth and seal tightly with elastic bands.
7. Place the jars in a dark area and which is room temperature. Store this for six to ten days. After day six you may begin sampling the kombucha. Never drink from the bottle as you risk introducing bacteria to the kombucha. You should taste both vinegar and sweet flavors. The longer that the tea ferments, the less sweet the kombucha will be.
8. Retain two cups of tea from this batch to use a starter for the next batch you plan to make. All you have to do is leave it in the jar(s) with the SCOBY. The rest of the liquid can be used for the second fermentation process.

Brewer's Notes

- When the SCOBY has grown to one-inch thick you can peel off a few layers to create a new, second SCOBY.
- During the first fermentation, you may experiment by making the tea using other varieties such as green tea, fruit teas, or oolong and white teas. If you are tempted to use fruitier teas, use three quarters in a recipe and one-quarter of black tea.

Third Step: Second Fermentation Process

This is where the magic begins and you have an opportunity to flavor your kombucha and add other ingredients such as herbs and fresh fruits.

Ingredients:

- Kombucha from your first fermentation.
- Sweetener of choice, which can include fruits, sugar, herbs, honey, and any other ingredients.
- Flip-top fermentation bottles, these are designed to hold the pressure.

Directions:

1. Using a sieve, strain the kombucha and transfer them into bottles, leaving 1 ½ inches at the top.

2. Add your chosen sweeteners, spices, or herbs and seal the bottles.
3. Place the jars in a dark area and which is room temperature. Store this for three to ten days.
4. Transfer the bottles into the refrigerator to begin the process of carbonation. You can remove any pieces of fruit and sweeteners before this if you wish.
5. These bottles can explode, so in order to know when the kombucha is ready for drinking use a tester bottle. All you do is transfer the same amount of kombucha into a plastic bottle and place it with the rest of the bottle in the refrigerator. When the plastic bottle is solid when squeezed you will know that the others are ready.
6. Burp your kombucha, gently unlock the lid to allow the pressure to escape. They are then ready to enjoy.
7. Return any burped kombucha bottles to the refrigerator to slow the fermentation process and so that you can continue to enjoy your batch of kombucha over the next few days.

Brewer's Notes

- Always open the bottles over the sink and have a towel at the ready as some can explode.
- Remember that the more fruit and sugar you add, the faster the kombucha will ferment.

Kombucha Making FAQ

Here are a few answers to a range of commonly asked questions.

Can I replace the sugar with Splenda or Stevia?

Unfortunately, you cannot substitute the sugar for anything else in the beginning phase. You will also not be consuming the whole one cup of sugar, as that portion is discarded. It is just the SCOBY you are after. Sugar is needed to feed the yeast and bacteria, by the time you drink your finished product the sugar content will be much lower.

Help, my SCOBY sank to the bottom of the jar!

Do not worry, each SCOBY takes on a life of its own. This is very normal, as long as there is no mold growing, it is fine.

Where do I store my kombucha?

You can store this in the refrigerator as it slows the fermentation process and kombucha served chilled is delicious.

Does the size of the SCOBY matter concerning the quantity of kombucha I plan to make?

The answer is no. Even a small SCOBY will allow one gallon of kombucha to ferment.

Chapter 5: Super Easy and Delicious Herbal Kombucha Recipes

Here are 25 recipes to kick-start your kombucha brewing journey!

Herbal Blends for Health

Try these five herbal blends when making the kombucha during the first fermentation process. The herbs can be interchanged with one another to make up more complex flavor profiles or can be further simplified.

Dandelion, Nettle, Yarrow, Raspberry Leaves, and Elderflower

A kombucha blend ideal for fighting off colds and flu.

Time: 5 to 10 days (includes cook and fermentation time)

Serving size: 16 cups

Prep time: 5 minutes

Cook time: 10 minutes

Ingredients:

- Dandelion
- Nettle
- Yarrow
- Raspberry leaves
- Elderflower

Directions:

1. When you have finished making your SCOBY and are ready to proceed with the first fermentation process simply add 1.5 to 1.8 ounces of dried herbs to the boiling water versus the black tea bags.
2. Continue with the kombucha process through the first and second fermentation processes.

Health benefits:

- **Dandelion:** Is great for digestion, supports those with diabetes, helps reduce water weight, and acts as a diuretic.
- **Nettle:** Helps to reduce inflammation and controls blood sugar levels.
- **Yarrow:** Yarrow has been known to stop heavy menstrual bleeding, lowers blood pressure, and helps improve blood circulation.
- **Raspberry leaves:** Have high levels of antioxidants which are important in fighting off colds and illnesses. They are rich in vitamin B and C, zinc, iron, and potassium.
- **Elderflower:** Elderflower is used to treat cold and flu, support those with diabetes, and those who struggle with constipation. It is also a diuretic and is suitable for those who are ill with bronchitis.

Useful tips:

1. The above-mentioned herbs should be added in equal parts.
2. Add more herbs if you enjoy a stronger tasting tea.

Ginger Root and Asian Pear

A kombucha tea that takes like champagne.

Time: 6 to 10 days (includes cook and fermentation time)

Serving size: 16 cups

Prep time: 5 minutes

Cook time: 10 minutes

Ingredients:

- Asian pears

- Ginger root

Directions:

1. When you have finished making your SCOBY and are ready to proceed with the first fermentation process simply add 1.5 to 1.8 ounces of dried herbs to the boiling water versus the black tea bags.
2. Continue with the kombucha process through the first and second fermentation processes.

Health benefits:

- **Asian pear:** These pears help to improve bone, blood, and cardiovascular health.
- **Ginger root:** Reduces oxidative stress and can stop free radicals from expanding.

Useful tips:

1. If you cannot find dried pear consider drying your own at home, or use freshly diced pear instead.
2. You may need to add more pear to the water to heighten the flavor.

Green Tea, Rosehip Peels, and Nettle Leaves

A kombucha blend ideal for those who want to fight the signs of aging and stave off heart disease.

Time: 6 to 10 days (includes cook and fermentation time)

Serving size: 16 cups.   **Prep time:** 5 minutes

Cook time: 10 minutes

Ingredients:

- Nettle leaves
- Rosehip peels
- Green tea leaves

Directions:

1. When you have finished making your SCOBY and are ready to proceed with the first fermentation process

simply add 1.5 to 1.8 ounces of dried herbs to the boiling water versus the black tea bags.
2. Continue with the kombucha process through the first and second fermentation processes.

Health benefits:

- **Nettle leaves:** Nettle contains powerful antioxidants that can protect the body from cell damage and aging.
- **Rosehip peels:** Rosehip fights the signs of aging and can protect against developing type 2 diabetes and heart disease.
- **Green tea:** Green tea is considered one of the best beverages that you can drink for your health. It can lower the risk of developing heart disease and cancer. It can aid weight loss and it can help improve brain function.

Useful tips:

1. The abovementioned herbs should be combined in equal parts.
2. Lessen the herbs for a softer tasting kombucha.

Yarrow, Lycopod, Dandelion, and Nettle

A herbal blend designed to support your liver, kidneys, and bladder.

Time: 6 to 10 days (includes cook and fermentation time)

Serving size: 16 cups   **Prep time:** 5 minutes

Cook time: 10 minutes

Ingredients:

- 3 parts yarrow
- 1 part lycopod
- 2 parts dandelion
- 1 part nettle

Directions:

1. When you have finished making your SCOBY and are ready to proceed with the first fermentation process

simply add 1.5 to 1.8 ounces of dried herbs to the boiling water versus the black tea bags.
2. Continue with the kombucha process through the first and second fermentation process.

Health benefits:

- **Yarrow:** Flavonoids present in yarrow are said to ease the symptoms of anxiety and depression.
- **Lycopod:** Lycopod or lycopodium is a traditional Chinese herb often used in medicines. It supports the digestive system, relaxes the muscles, and has anti-inflammatory properties.
- **Dandelion:** Dandelion, especially incorporated into teas and kombucha can help prevent urinary tract infections as well as support the kidney and bladder.
- **Nettle:** Nettle is also known to flush away bad bacteria that occur in the urinary tract and help support the function of medicines that are prescribed to treat urinary tract infections.

Useful tip:

1. You may consider using ginger, goldenrod, or marshmallow root in place of the dandelion and nettle. These three herbs are known for supporting the kidneys and bladder.

Cinnamon, Rosehip, and Elderberry

Drink your way to a happy, healthy heart.

Time: 6 to 10 days (includes cook and fermentation time)

Serving size: 16 cups   **Prep time:** 5 minutes

Cook time: 10 minutes

Ingredients:

- Cinnamon chips
- Rosehip
- Elderberry

Directions:

1. When you have finished making your SCOBY and are ready to proceed with the first fermentation process simply add 1.5 to 1.8 ounces of dried herbs to the boiling water versus the black tea bags.
2. Continue with the kombucha process through the first and second fermentation processes.

Health benefits:

- **Cinnamon chips:** Can boost your sensitivity towards insulin and have a strong anti-diabetic effect on the body.
- **Rosehip:** Helps support the skin's protective layer that guards against pathogens. It also stimulates the production of white blood cells which protect you from infections.
- **Elderberry:** Elderberry can positively impact your mood and can lessen stress and anxiety.

Useful tip:

1. Feel free to substitute the cinnamon chips for ginger root which helps aid digestion. You may also substitute the chips for hibiscus flowers, known to improve the health of the liver and lower blood fat levels.

Woodruff, Yarrow, Dandelion, Nettle Leaves, and Chickweed

This blend is designed to help lower blood pressure and support those who have type 2 diabetes.

Time: 6 to 10 days (includes cook and fermentation time)

Serving size: 16 cups   **Prep time:** 5 minutes

Cook time: 10 minutes

Ingredients:

- Woodruff
- Yarrow
- Dandelion
- Nettle leaves
- Chickweed

Directions:

1. When you have finished making your SCOBY and are ready to proceed with the first fermentation process simply add 1.5 to 1.8 ounces of dried herbs to the boiling water versus the black tea bags.
2. Continue with the kombucha process through the first and second fermentation processes.

Health benefits:

- **Woodruff:** Woodruff treats blood circulation issues and can bring on sleep for those who suffer from insomnia. Its properties also guard against liver, stomach, liver and gallbladder related disorders.

- **Yarrow:** Yarrow provides support to those who suffer from brain-related disorders such as Alzheimer's and Parkinson's. It may also ease any inflammation related to the brain.
- **Dandelion:** Dandelion may reduce cholesterol levels in people who have elevated levels of bad cholesterol in their system. This may decrease the likelihood of developing heart disease later on in life.
- **Nettle leaves:** Nettle is said to lower the blood sugar levels of people who suffer from type 2 diabetes.
- **Chickweed:** Chickweed can help those who may be struggling with a buildup of phlegm, especially when ill. It is a good expectorant, which means that it is efficient in loosening phlegm.

Useful tips:

1. The abovementioned herbs should be combined in equal parts.

2. Rosemary and lemon balm can be included into this recipe too. Both of these herbs help support cognitive health.

Strawberry Leaves, Blackberry Leaves, Raspberry Leaves, and Black Currant Leaves

A herbal blend ideal for women of all ages. The ingredients are powered to support women's health.

Time: 6 to 10 days (includes cook and fermentation time)

Serving size: 16 cups

Prep time: 5 minutes

Cook time: 10 minutes

Ingredients:

- Strawberry leaves
- Blackberry leaves
- Raspberry leaves
- Black currant leaves

Directions:

1. When you have finished making your SCOBY and are ready to proceed with the first fermentation process simply add 1.5 to 1.8 ounces of dried herbs to the boiling water versus the black tea bags.
2. Continue with the kombucha process through the first and second fermentation processes.

Health benefits:

- **Strawberry leaves:** Strawberry leaves contain illness preventing properties, and are high in antioxidants. They are all known for their anti-inflammatory properties.
- **Blackberry leaves:** Blackberry leaves serve as a diuretic, and ease swelling and pain. They also help with any fluid retention and support those who struggle with gout.
- **Raspberry leaves:** Raspberry leaves are also known to support women's health issues, stabilize hormones, and help ease nausea.
- **Black currant leaves:** Contain a high amount of antioxidants and are known to strengthen the immune system and soothe the symptoms of flu.

Useful tips:

1. The abovementioned herbs should be combined in equal parts.
2. You could also supplement any of the leaves with a batch of blueberry leaves. Blueberry leaves are pivotal in supporting brain function and contain high amounts of vitamin C.

Fruit-Infused Herbal Drinks

Basil and Strawberry Kombucha

A fresh, fragrant kombucha tea ideal for the summertime.

Time: 96 hours and 35 minutes (includes cook and fermentation time)

Serving size: 16 cups

Prep time: 35 minutes

Cook time: Four days of fermentation.

Ingredients:

- 1 cup fresh basil leaves
- 2 cups strawberries
- ½ cup water
- ½ cup white sugar
- 3 gallons homemade herbal kombucha

Directions:

1. Brew your first batch of homemade kombucha. When it is ready to enter the second fermentation process follow the directions below.
2. In a saucepan over medium heat add the water, sugar, basil and strawberries. Bring this to a boil then allow to simmer for further 10 minutes. Remove from heat, and using a fork, mash the strawberries. Allow to cool to room temperature.

3. In a large jar add half the basil and strawberry mixture and half the homemade kombucha. Stir well.
4. Pour this mixture into your flip-top bottles, fill the bottle to three-quarters of the way. Then evenly divide the remaining basil and strawberry mixture between the bottles.
5. Seal the bottles and allow them to rest in a dark, warm place for between two and four days. Place them into the refrigerator and allow to chill.
6. When ready to serve, burp the bottles, strain the mixture and enjoy!

Health benefits:

- **Basil:** Basil is a rich source of vitamin A, C and K and is high in iron. It helps to fight inflammation, is good for digestion, and detoxifies the body.
- **Strawberry:** Strawberries protect your heart and up the levels of good cholesterol. It can also protect those from cancer and can lower blood pressure.

Useful tips:

1. Use filtered water when making your kombucha.
2. You may consider using one cup strawberries and one cup blueberries for another flavor combination.

Ginger and Blueberry Kombucha

Keep the aches and pains away with this zingy kombucha tea.

Time: 73 hours and 10 minutes (Including cook and fermentation time)

Serving size: 16 cups

Prep time: 10 minutes

Cook time: 1 hour

Ingredients:

- 1 ½ cups water
- 1 cup blueberries
- 2 tbsp white sugar
- 1 tbsp fresh ginger, shredded
- 1 gallon homemade herbal kombucha

Directions:

1. In a large saucepan, over medium heat add the water, sugar, ginger and blueberries. Bring the mixture to a boil. Then simmer for 10 minutes.
2. Remove from heat and, using a wooden spoon, squash the blueberries. Allow this mixture to cool down to room temperature.
3. Take the SCOBY out of your homemade kombucha and retain one cup of your homemade kombucha.

Transfer the blueberry mixture to the remainder of your homemade kombucha.
4. Using a sieve strain this mixture and pour the tea into your flip-top bottles, leaving an inch near the top. Store in a warm, dark area from one to three days then transfer to the refrigerator.
5. When ready to drink, strain the mixture once more before serving.

Health benefits:

- **Ginger:** Ginger treats nausea and can reduce muscle pain and soreness. It also has powerful anti-inflammatory properties which can help ease the symptoms of those who suffer from osteoarthritis.
- **Blueberry:** Blueberries are important in supporting brain function and are recommended for those who struggle with dementia.

Useful tips:

1. When pouring the blueberry mixture over to the kombucha do so slowly as it may foam and bubble up.

Mint and Peach Kombucha

A refreshing kombucha drink with a dash of mint.

Time: 73 hours and 10 minutes (Including cook and fermentation time)

Serving size: 16 cups

Prep time: 10 minutes

Cook time: 1 hour

Ingredients:

- 2 tbsp white sugar
- 2 tbsp fresh mint leaves
- 1 ½ cups water
- 1 cup peaches, peeled, pitted and diced
- 1 gallon homemade kombucha

Directions:

1. In a large saucepan, over medium heat add the water, sugar, mint and peaches. Bring the mixture to a boil. Then simmer for 10 minutes.
2. Remove from the heat and, using a wooden spoon, squash the peaches. Allow this mixture to cool down to room temperature.
3. Take the SCOBY out of your homemade kombucha and retain one cup of your homemade kombucha.

Transfer the blueberry mixture to the remainder of your homemade kombucha.
4. Using a sieve, strain this mixture and pour the tea into your flip-top bottles, leaving an inch near the top. Store in a warm, dark area from one to three days then transfer to the refrigerator.
5. When ready to drink, strain the mixture once more then serve.

Health benefits:

- **Mint:** Mint may help ease the symptoms of irritable bowel syndrome and can relieve indigestion.
- **Peach:** Peaches protect your skin and aid in digestion too.

Useful tip:

1. You could choose to use apricots instead of the diced peaches. Apricots are also helpful in improving skin health and also promotes gut health.

Kombucha Lemonade

A refreshing take on the traditional kombucha tea.

Time: 11 minutes

Serving size: 4 cups

Prep time: 6 minutes

Cook time: 5 minutes

Ingredients:

- 1 cup water
- ½ cup lemon juice
- 1 tbsp coconut sugar
- 2 cups homemade kombucha
- Half a handful of fresh mint leaves

Directions:

1. In a large pitcher combine the homemade kombucha with the lemon juice.
2. In a separate bowl, combine the coconut sugar and water until the sugar has dissolved.
3. Add the sugar and water mixture to the kombucha mixture. Add ice, stir through fresh mint leaves then serve!

Health benefits:

- **Lemon:** Lemon is high in vitamin C and improves the quality of your skin.
- **Mint:** Mint can help ease the symptoms of colds and flu and it can mask bad breath.

Useful tips:

1. You could substitute the lemon for orange juice instead. Oranges are high in vitamin C and are beneficial for those who are battling with colds and flu.
2. For an extra kick, consider adding a few strips of lemon peel into your drink.
3. Consider giving your drink a stir with a few stems of lavender.

Rosemary and Citrus Kombucha

A kombucha drink loaded with vitamin C.

Time: 3 days and 30 minutes (includes cook and fermentation time)

Serving size: 8 cups

Prep time: 25 minutes

Cook time: 5 minutes

Ingredients:

- Zest of one lemon
- 3 sprigs fresh rosemary
- 1 juiced ruby grapefruit
- 64 oz. homemade kombucha

Directions:

1. Juice the grapefruit and set this aside. Zest the lemon in a separate bowl.
2. Combine the grapefruit, lemon zest and rosemary in a large pitcher.
3. Add the homemade kombucha to the jar and give it all a good stir.
4. Cover the top of the jar with a few layers of cheesecloth and secure with an elastic band.
5. Allow this to sit for three days in a warm, dark area.

6. Remove from storage, give it a good stir, strain and then serve.

Health benefits:

- **Grapefruit:** Grapefruit benefits your immune system and improves heart health. It also aids weight loss and suppresses the appetite.
- **Rosemary:** Rosemary can prevent the brain from rapidly aging and provide neurological protection. It also enhances concentration and memory.

Useful tips:

1. If you would like for your kombucha to be fizzy, consider bottling the kombucha after straining it. Continue to store it in a warm, dark area for another five to seven days before moving it over into the refrigerator.

Spiced Pear

There is nothing that beats the aroma of spice pear. This makes it one of my favorite recipes.

Time: 72 hours and 20 minutes (including cook and fermentation time)

Serving size: 8 servings   **Prep time:** 10 minutes

Cook time: 10 minutes

Ingredients:

- 4 cloves, whole
- 1 pear, shredded
- 2 tsp ginger, shredded
- ½ gallon homemade kombucha (from first fermentation)

Directions:

1. Share the cloves, ginger, and pear evenly into four flip-top fermentation bottles. Top the ingredients off with the kombucha from your first fermentation. Leave 2 inches at the top.
2. Place in a warm, dark area for three to 10 days until it reaches the carbonation level that you enjoy.
3. Place in the refrigerator, when ready to drink, strain the kombucha then serve.

Health benefits:

- **Cloves:** Cloves kill off bad bacteria and can help regulate blood sugar levels and improve both liver and bone health.
- **Pear:** Pear is rich in nutrients, minerals and vitamins that protect against developing certain cancers and diabetes. It also promotes good gut health.
- **Ginger:** Ginger is known to help ease respiratory problems and may even relieve discomfort brought on by menstruation.

Useful tip:

1. You can make plain pear kombucha by omitting the ginger and clove.

Kombucha Smoothies

Honey and Ginger Smoothie

A great way to get your kombucha in!

Time: 10 minutes

Serving size: 4 cups

Prep time: 5 minutes

Cook time: 5 minutes

Ingredients:

- 1 cup frozen blackberries
- 1 cup frozen, cubed mango
- ½ frozen banana
- Juice from ½ a lemon
- ½ cup honey
- 1 ¼ cup homemade kombucha
- 1 knob ginger, shredded

Directions:

1. Place all the ingredients into a blender or food processor, pulse until well combined and smooth. Serve and enjoy!

Health benefits:

- **Blackberries:** Blackberries support oral health and hygiene. They are rich in vitamin C and K and can help boost brain health.
- **Mango:** Mangos help fight off cancers, they maintain your cholesterol and they help alkalize your body.
- **Banana:** They are rich in potassium which helps regulate blood pressure and maintains a healthy heart. They can help fight gastrointestinal issues and are a source of energy.
- **Honey:** Honey improves the levels of cholesterol within the body, it can also lower blood pressure and improve the health of your heart.
- **Ginger:** Ginger helps soothe muscle pain and soreness. It helps to ease those who experience nausea and is especially effective in helping ease the symptoms of morning sickness.

Useful tip:

1. Honey is an optional extra in this recipe. You may add your own sweetener such as maple syrup. Or add Stevia afterward to taste.

Go for Green Smoothie

Get all your greens and more with one serving of this smoothie.

Time: 12 minutes

Serving size: 2 servings

Prep time: 7 minutes

Cook time: 5 minutes

Ingredients:

- 1 scoop protein powder
- 1 cup ice
- 1 cup homemade kombucha
- 2 tbsp frozen mango
- 2 tbsp ground flaxseed
- 1 apple, diced
- 1 avocado, peeled and pitted
- ½ cup fresh dill
- 2 handfuls fresh spinach leaves

Directions:

1. Place all the ingredients into a blender or food processor, pulse until well combined and smooth. Serve and enjoy!

Health benefits:

- **Mango:** Mango cleanses the skin and helps support eye health.
- **Flaxseed:** Flaxseed is rich in omega-three fats, is a source of dietary fiber and improves cholesterol levels.
- **Apple:** Apple promotes good gut bacteria.
- **Avocado:** Avocados are high in vitamins C, E, K and B6. They are also pivotal in minimizing the damage to eye tissue.
- **Spinach:** Spinach contains large amounts of iron and supports the body by transporting oxygen through the body which is important for overall health.
- **Dill:** Dill helps the body to resist infection and is important in maintaining healthy, strong bones.

Useful tips:

1. Ice is an optional extra and so is the protein powder.
2. Buy fresh fruit and store them in the freezer for when you want to make this smoothie instead of buying pre-frozen goods.
3. Replace the dill with fresh basil instead. Basil fights off free radicals that cause aging and illness.

Berry, Banana, Jasmine, and Lavender Smoothie

Loved up with this "berrylicious" smoothie!

Time: 10 minutes

Serving size: 2 servings

Prep time: 5 minutes

Cook time: 5 minutes

Ingredients:

- 1 cup homemade kombucha
- 1 frozen banana
- 1 cup frozen, mixed berries (strawberry, blueberry, and raspberry)
- 1 pinch of lavender
- 1 pinch of jasmine

Directions:

1. Place all the ingredients into a blender or food processor, pulse until well combined and smooth. Serve and enjoy!

Health benefits:

- **Banana:** They produce red blood cells and metabolize amino acids. They also remove any

unwanted chemicals that lodge themselves in the liver and kidneys.
- **Strawberry:** Strawberries help reduce oxidative stress.
- **Blueberry:** Blueberries help manage type 2 diabetes, prevent cancer and support mental health.
- **Raspberry:** Raspberries fight against cancer, age-related decline and circulatory illnesses.
- **Lavender:** Lavender stabilizes heart rate, and can lower blood pressure. It also has calming properties and can uplift your mood.
- **Jasmine:** Jasmine may protect individuals against developing Parkinson's disease and Alzheimer's. It also lowers the risk of developing type 2 diabetes and specific cancers.

Useful tips:

1. Consider using a green tea based homemade kombucha as a base for this smoothie.
2. You may choose to use one variety of berry instead, which is fine too.

Ginger, Thyme, and Blueberry Smoothie

Refreshing and healthy, all in one serving!

Time: 10 minutes

Serving size: 1 serving

Prep time: 5 minutes

Cook time: 5 minutes

Ingredients:

- 1 knob ginger, shredded
- 1 cup frozen blueberries
- 1 frozen banana
- 1 cup homemade kombucha
- 1 pinch of fresh thyme

Directions:

1. Place all the ingredients into a blender or food processor, pulse until well combined and smooth. Serve and enjoy!

Health benefits:

- **Ginger:** Ginger ease inflammation and therefore helpful for those who suffer from arthritis. It is also rich in antiviral properties.

- **Blueberries:** Did you know that one cup of blueberries can provide 24% of a person's daily intake of vitamin C?
- **Banana:** Bananas provide 13% of your required manganese intake. Manganese supports your body by producing collagen and helps guard against free radicals which cause early aging.
- **Thyme:** Improves your immunity and can protect you against getting colds and flu. It also has a positive effect on moods.

Useful tip:

1. Feel free to substitute the thyme for fresh rosemary or lavender.

Apple and Dandelion Smoothie

An herbaceous fueled smoothie filled with powerful ingredients.

Time: 10 minutes

Serving size: 2 servings

Prep time: 5 minutes

Cook time: 5 minutes

Ingredients:

- 2 cups homemade kombucha
- ½ cup water
- 4 oz. fresh spinach leaves
- 2 apples, diced
- 4 oz. fresh dandelion, diced
- 2 tsp barley grass powder

Directions:

1. Place all the ingredients into a blender or food processor, pulse until well combined and smooth. Serve and enjoy!

Health benefits:

- **Spinach:** Spinach restores energy and remarkably improves the quality of blood within the body.

- **Apple:** Apples are high in fiber that may be beneficial in maintaining body weight and are linked to decreasing the likelihood of developing type 2 diabetes.
- **Dandelion:** Dandelion may reduce your risk of developing cancer. Specifically colon, liver and pancreatic cancers.
- **Barley grass:** Barley grass boosts the immune system and kills off bad bacteria. It is said to fuel the metabolism and lowers excess acidity.

Useful tips:

1. You may be encouraged to add half a tablespoon of spirulina to boost the health benefits of this smoothie.

Leftover SCOBY Recipes
Cookie Dough

Shhh... do not tell the kids!

Time: 15 minutes

Serving size: 4 cups

Prep time: 10 minutes

Cook time: 5 minutes

Ingredients:

- 1 pinch of Maldon salt
- ½ cup chocolate chips
- 1 ½ cup sprouted spelt flour
- ¾ cup oats

- ½ cup coconut sugar
- ½ cup coconut oil
- 1 tsp vanilla extract
- ¼ cup SCOBY, puréed

Directions:

1. In a large mixing bowl combine the vanilla, sugar, coconut oil and SCOBY puree.
2. Add the oats, flour and salt. Combine well.
3. Fold in the chocolate chips. Serve and enjoy.

Health benefits:

Oats are rich in fiber and lower bad cholesterol levels. Coconut boosts the metabolism and supports bone health.

Useful tips:

1. Feel free to mix through a cup of nuts. Serve in the mornings with a cup of yogurt. The kids will be none the wiser.
2. Store this cookie dough mixture in an airtight container in the refrigerator.

Probiotic Energy Balls

This is a delicious way to incorporate prebiotics and probiotics into your diet when on the go.

Time: 1 hour and 10 minutes

Serving size: 16 energy balls

Prep time: 10 minutes

Cook time: 1 hour

Ingredients:

- ¼ cup SCOBY, puréed
- 3 tbsp honey
- 1 tsp vanilla extract
- ½ cup peanut butter
- 1 cup oatmeal
- ⅓ cup dried cherries

Directions:

1. In a medium bowl, combine the cherries, oatmeal, peanut butter, and SCOBY puree.
2. Place the mixture into the refrigerator and allow it to firm up.
3. Using a teaspoon, scoop some of the dough into the palm of your hand and then roll into a small ball. Continue to do so until your mixture is finished.

4. Store them in the refrigerator and enjoy over time, yum!

Health benefits:

Cherries lower hypertension and prevent diseases related to the heart. Nuts are just as important for heart health as they contain vitamin B1, that is responsible for the functioning of your nervous system, heart, and muscles.

Useful tips:

1. You may substitute the peanut butter with an alternative nut butter such as almond or cashew.
2. You are welcome to swap out the dried cherries for either raisins or dried cranberries.

Garlic Dressing

A garlicky dressing best served over a leafy green salad.

Time: 15 minutes

Serving size: 2 cups

Prep time: 10 minutes

Cook time: 5 minutes

Ingredients:

- 1 pinch of salt
- 1 pinch of black, ground pepper
- 1 tbsp mustard
- 1 tbsp honey

- 1 cup extra-virgin olive oil
- 3 tbsp water
- 6 cloves of garlic, minced
- ⅓ cup SCOBY, puréed

Directions:

1. Place all the ingredients into a blender or food processor, pulse until well combined and smooth. Serve and enjoy!

Health benefits:

Garlic may lower the risk of developing heart disease and is said to combat both colds and flu. Olive oil may reduce the risk of suffering from a stroke and boasts powerful antioxidant and anti-inflammatory properties.

Useful tips:

1. Up the flavor by adding a pinch of fresh flat-leaf parsley, oregano and sage.

SCOBY Popsicles

Make these SCOBY popsicles during the summer months. This is a delicious and simple way in which to get your probiotics in.

Time: 4 hours and 10 minutes (includes freezing time)

Serving size: 4 popsicles

Prep time: 10 minutes

Cook time: 4 hours

Ingredients:

- 2 tsp liquid stevia
- 3 tbsp of homemade kombucha
- ½ cup SCOBY, puréed
- ¾ cup mixed berries

Directions:

1. Place all the ingredients into a blender or food processor, pulse until well combined and smooth.
2. Transfer the mixture into popsicle molds, then freeze for up to four hours.
3. When set, use a bit of hot water to get them out of their molds.

Health benefits:

Apart from the probiotic benefits a mixed berry smoothie will boost cognitive function and your immune system

Useful tip:

1. You are welcome to substitute the mixed berries for other fruits. Bear in mind the freezing times may differ.

Herbal Kombucha Cocktails

Vodka Kombucha Zinger

A class drink with a zing.

Time: 5 minutes

Serving size: 1 serving

Prep time: 2 minutes

Cook time: 3 minutes

Ingredients:

- 1 sprig of fresh rosemary
- 3 oz. of homemade kombucha
- 1 oz. vodka
- 1 tsp lime juice, to taste

Directions:

1. Pour the kombucha into a tall glass, over ice. Add the vodka, lime juice and rosemary, then serve.

Useful tip:

1. Consider using a green tea based homemade kombucha for this recipe.

Moscow Mule

The real deal with a twist.

Time: 5 minutes

Serving size: 1 serving

Prep time: 2 minutes

Cook time: 3 minutes

Ingredients:

- 1 sprig of fresh mint
- 6 oz. of homemade kombucha
- 1.5 oz. vodka
- Juice of ½ a lime

Directions:

2. Pour the kombucha into a tall glass, over ice. Add the vodka, lime juice and mint then serve.

Useful tips:

1. Consider using a ginger-based homemade kombucha for this recipe.

Cranberry Mule

Time to get festive with a take on an old classic.

Time: 5 minutes

Serving size: 1 serving

Prep time: 2 minutes

Cook time: 3 minutes

Ingredients:

- Crushed ice
- ¼ cup fresh cranberries
- 1 orange slice
- 1 sprig of fresh rosemary
- 1 oz. lime juice
- 2 oz. orange juice
- 2 oz. dry gin
- 6 oz. homemade kombucha

Directions:

1. Fill half the glass with crushed ice.
2. Follow by adding the kombucha, gin, orange juice, and lime juice.
3. Top with fresh cranberries, a slice of orange and rosemary sprig.

Useful tip:

1. Swap out the lime juice for orange juice or alternatively, use grapefruit juice and slices.

Conclusion

Currently, there are studies and research underway to further investigate the many health benefits of kombucha. Many people are choosing to drink kombucha to help improve the health of their gut, relieve the symptoms of stress and depression and treat inflammation.

Though it has gained a strong following, it is important that if you are taking any medications or pregnant to consult with your healthcare provider to make sure that kombucha is safe to drink.

Overall kombucha has a range of health benefits that are hard to ignore and will surely become a fixed item on grocery store shelves for years to come.

Happy brewing!

THANKS FOR READING THIS BOOK

If you found this material very helpful, feel free to share it with your friends. You can also help others find it for me to encourage me to continue writing books you love reading.

***

I really appreciate you taking the time to read my book.

Regards,

Kevin Curt

Printed in Great Britain
by Amazon